SUPERCRAFT
CHRISTMAS

SUPERCRAFT
CHRISTMAS

Sophie Pester
Catharina Bruns

Contents

"A festival of joy and friendship it shall be. Because friendship is the finest gift a person can give."

Author unknown

Introduction

'Tis the season once more! As the first Advent lights are lit,
it's time to turn your thoughts and fingers to making
the Christmas festivities at home truly special
for you and your friends and family.

This unique winter festival is a time for contemplation and togetherness, but also a celebration of special wishes, gifts, and presents. That is probably why Christmas is such a great time to be creative; there is no better way to express your love and affection than with home-made gifts and personalized decorations. As you will see, the yuletide spirit can be created in just a few easy steps. What would Christmas be without the familiar evocative aromas, the festive ornaments, and the twinkling eyes of excited children having fun?

This book is crammed with wonderful ideas for a creative Christmas: from DIY decorations and gifts, to imaginative gift-wrapping ideas, and super-quick last-minute projects. Because – quite honestly – who has time to spare at this time of year? To guarantee a festive mood without the preparations degenerating into a total stress melt-down, we have been particularly careful to design the projects here to be simple to achieve while still being impressive. Most are not too time-consuming and can be made over the Christmas period with materials you may well already have tucked away in cupboards at home. We want to inspire you to make lovely little offerings for your friends and family, and to conjure up a relaxed and beautiful holiday by getting in touch with your inner creative spirit. Many of the crafting ideas in the book can also be made with children. After all, the most important thing at Christmas is to find time for each other and to make things nice and cosy!

Wishing you a wonderful Christmas,

Sophie & Catharina

Basic equipment

Whatever the craft activity, having the correct tools is half the battle! To make sure the projects in this book run smoothly and turn out well, here is a brief list of kit you may need.

We have made sure our projects can be achieved without expensive or unusual tools. The equipment used is generally found in any creative household or, if not, is widely available in shops. As a DIY enthusiast you will probably already own much of it.

The following will set you up to take on any of the craft ideas in this book:

∗ scissors
∗ pens
∗ calligraphy pen
∗ craft glue and glue stick
∗ adhesive tape and masking tape
∗ various paintbrushes
∗ acrylic paints
∗ wire
∗ little sponges
∗ thread and sewing machine
∗ cord, wool, and embroidery threads
∗ sewing and embroidery needles
∗ crochet hooks and knitting needles
∗ pins
∗ iron
∗ nail varnish
∗ hole punch
∗ pliers
∗ cutting board
∗ ruler (with steel edge)
∗ scalpel, craft knife, or cutter
∗ glue gun
∗ linoleum cutters
∗ linoleum ink roller

∗ Tip ∗

You can tell how difficult a project is by the number of little stars above the list of materials. One star means it is super-easy; for three stars you will need a bit more time.

Decorating

●

Festive ornaments are as much a part of Christmas as mince pies and Santa Claus. Creative decorative projects are fun, and will get you in the yuletide mood as you work...

Marbled tree baubles

Every Christmas the same question crops up: what colour scheme should we choose for the tree decorations? This year, you can create your own customized combination.

Bespoke baubles are absolutely perfect if you are looking for Christmas tree decorations which will stand out from the classic red, but are unusual while still being festive and fashionable. They are quick to make and, of course, you can choose whatever colours your heart desires.

How it's done:

1. Attach a piece of string to a Christmas tree bauble. Fill a large bowl with enough lukewarm water to completely submerge the bauble.

2. Add a few drops from each of the bottles of nail varnish to the water. The nail varnish will form a thin, colourful film on the surface of the water.

✳✳❋
🕐 *2 minutes per bauble, plus drying time*

You will need:
✳ *colourful thread or string*
✳ *scissors*
✳ *white Christmas tree baubles in various sizes*
✳ *large bowl*
✳ *nail varnish in 2 colours, here: orange and lilac*

3. Now immerse the bauble completely in the bowl, holding the cap and ring to push it under water.

4. A thin layer of nail varnish will coat the bauble. Hang it up to dry for a couple of hours.

Evergreen garland

This string of fairy lights is a properly festive project, using fragrant coniferous branches and tree ornaments.

* ❄ ❄
🕐 *1–2 hours*

You will need:

* *scissors*
* *evergreen branches*
* *long chain of small fairy lights on green wire*
* *green thread or wire*
* *Christmas tree decorations*

If you don't fancy having a Christmas tree, or haven't got space for one, you can make yourself a beautiful alternative with this garland. It is guaranteed to create a celebratory atmosphere and can be hung up around a doorway. The presents will feel quite at home underneath!

How it's done:

1. Cut individual offshoots from the evergreen branches and attach them to the fairy lights using little pieces of thread or wire. Try to leave no gaps; the lights should seem to be shining out from a garland of pine twigs.

2. Now hang up the chain, attaching it securely to a door frame, or to a fireplace, or other chosen spot.

3. Finally, decorate the garland with Christmas tree decorations, such as baubles and stars.

* Tip *

By using outdoor fairy lights and weatherproof decorations, you can also use this idea to adorn your balcony or garden.

Festive floral sphere

This beautiful ornament works both inside and in a sheltered spot outdoors, and you don't need to be a florist to make it.

These lush green orbs are easy to make and are a quick way of embellishing any room. If you dampen the floral foam, the plants will stay fresh for longer. Use any festive greenery you have; those listed here are just suggestions.

How it's done:

1. Lay out a 160cm (5ft) length of wire, then double it up. Push this, loop first, all the way through a foam ball.

2. Bend and twist the wire loop to create a hook. This will enable you to hang up your ornament later.

3. Cut your chosen twigs, flowers, and berries into little pieces. Attach strawflower pins to the little gold bells. Poke all the pieces into the ball all the way around. Start with the greenery, fixing a few of the larger leaves in place with pins so they don't stick out too much, then distribute the flowers, berries, and bells in between. Hang using the hook or the long ends of the wire.

∗ ∗ ❋

🕐 *1 hour per sphere*

You will need:
∗ *thick gold-coloured wire*
∗ *2 floral foam spheres, 10cm (4in) and 15cm (6in) in diameter*
∗ *scissors*
∗ *eucalyptus branches*
∗ *sea holly* (Eryngium planum)
∗ *St John's wort with berries*
∗ *ivy berries*
∗ *false cypress* (Chamaecyparis) *branches*
∗ *floristry strawflower pins*
∗ *little gold bells*
∗ *pins with flat metal heads*

Warning:
Many berries are poisonous and can be left out or replaced by other plant varieties, if you prefer.

Winter wreath

You can make a floral wreath from gypsophila in no time at all. It looks fantastic hanging in a modern home and conjures up a wintry mood, even if you prefer your Christmas decorations on the minimalist side.

✳ ❅ ❅

🕐 *30 minutes*

You will need:

* *scissors*
* *gypsophila*
* *white metal ring, 20–30cm (8–12in) in diameter*
* *thin wire*
* *ribbon, for hanging*

Gypsophila, or baby's breath, is really easy to work with, and the wreath will look great even without any additional decorative elements. Of course, if you like, you can titivate it a bit more with little baubles or bells.

How it's done:

1. Cut little offshoots from the gypsophila, then take 1 or 2 of these together, lay the stems along the metal ring and wrap thin wire around them 3–4 times.

2. Continue attaching flower sprigs until the entire ring is covered, erring on the side of generosity and leaving no gaps.

3. Securely hang the wreath up in your chosen spot with a length of ribbon.

* Tip *

Gypsophila still looks good when it has dried out, so the wreath can happily stay hanging in your home for a long time.

Christmas pot pourri

One of the best things about the festive period is the scents which waft through your house, whether from baking biscuits, pine needles, citrus, or Christmas spices.

This natural room fragrance adds immeasurably to the anticipation of Christmas and creates a homely atmosphere. An aromatic decoration for a cosy time of year.

How it's done:

1. When you next go on a woodland walk, bring home a couple of lovely evergreen twigs and some pine cones and put them in a large bowl. If there is some resin coming out of the twigs and cones, all the better. The resin contains particularly high quantities of essential oils and has a wonderful coniferous aroma. Add a couple of little yuletide logs, too, if you like.

2. The perfect partners for these fresh woody scents are oranges, mandarins, lemons, apples, cinnamon sticks, and walnuts. A particularly special addition to the festive fragrances can be created by including a bergamot orange. This is a citrus fruit which tea drinkers may well be familiar with: Earl Grey tea is flavoured with bergamot oil. To help release the scent of the bergamot, carefully carve shallow incisions in the zest using a knife.

✱ ❆ ❆
🕐 *10 minutes*

You will need:
- *evergreen twigs*
- *pine cones*
- *large bowl*
- *logs (optional)*
- *oranges*
- *mandarins*
- *lemons*
- *apples*
- *cinnamon sticks*
- *walnuts*
- *bergamot (optional)*
- *knife (optional)*

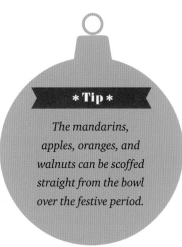

✱ Tip ✱

The mandarins, apples, oranges, and walnuts can be scoffed straight from the bowl over the festive period.

Dried flower Advent wreath

If you are not a fan of traditional Advent wreaths, this alternative, understated option might be the perfect solution for you.

✳✳❉

🕓 *30 minutes*

You will need:

* ✳ *scissors*
* ✳ *hydrangea flowers, fresh or dried*
* ✳ *floral foam ring with waterproof base, 40–50cm (16–20in) in diameter*
* ✳ *4 white candles*

"Thousands of candles can be lighted from a single candle, and the life of the single candle will not be shortened. Happiness never decreases by being shared"

Buddha

It's incredibly easy to make this wonderful wreath using dried hydrangea flowers. The Advent candles are simply positioned in the middle. When Advent is over, the wreath can still be used as a decoration. It keeps for a long time and is a beautiful addition to your coffee table, or can be hung on a wall.

How it's done:

1. Depending on their size, cut the flower heads to create smaller bunches. Stick these bunches into the foam ring. Continue until you've completely covered the ring. Finally, place the candles in the centre of your wreath.

2. We made our wreath from flowers which we picked in the autumn and dried ourselves. If you want to use fresh flowers, you can soak the foam ring in water beforehand. Later it can just be left standing, without needing more water, and the arrangement will slowly dry out over time; the flowers will still look amazing.

Christmas tree chains

Didn't there used to be more tinsel?
Yes... but these days we want some fresh ideas
for the Christmas tree.

These fun chains made from beads, bells, and popcorn are perfect if you want a natural look for your tree. Threading the chains is a guaranteed evening of fun for all the family. Just be careful when you're piercing the popcorn... and don't scoff all your working materials.

How it's done:

1. For each chain, cut a 2m (6½ft) piece of string.

2. Use the needle to thread popcorn, beads, pompoms, and bells, in whatever order you choose. You can also make the chain from a single material, like the pompom chain at the bottom of the tree in the picture on the left. Don't use freshly made popcorn, because it crumbles and is really tricky to thread. Leftover popcorn from a previous evening's film viewing is perfect!

✳ ✳ ✳

🕐 *30 minutes per chain*

You will need:

* ✳ *scissors*
* ✳ *string or thread*
* ✳ *thin needle*
* ✳ *salted popcorn (a few days old)*
* ✳ *beads*
* ✳ *white pompoms in various sizes*
* ✳ *little bells*

Snowflake tablecloth

Even if today's Christmas celebrations have been modernized, we still like to be reminded of the old traditions.

One of those long-established customs is the Christmas tablecloth, sewn by great-grandma and handed down through the generations. So we had to give this book a similar project. An embroidered tablecloth is a wonderful "forever" heirloom that children, grandchildren, and great-grandchildren will still be able to enjoy in years to come.

How it's done:

1. First transfer the embroidery design on to the tablecloth. To do this, poke through the holes in the template on to the fabric with a pencil or transfer marker (follow the marker packet instructions for use). If you sketch the design first with a transfer marker, the pattern can be removed later with cold water.

2. Next, join up the individual pre-sketched points using simple stitches (see pp108–109).

✶✶❋

☺ *depending on the size of the tablecloth, the design, and your level of diligence, 5 hours to 50 years*

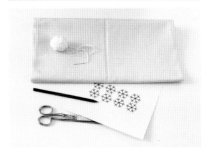

You will need:

* ✶ *template (see p122)*
* ✶ *white cotton or linen tablecloth*
* ✶ *sharp pencil, or transfer marker*
* ✶ *white embroidery thread*
* ✶ *embroidery needle*
* ✶ *scissors*

Did you know that, in Poland, the Christmas dinner table is always laid with an extra place setting? This is a sign of hospitality. It means that an unexpected guest will always have a seat at the table.

Pompom door wreath

Wool baubles and tassels lend a dash of warmth and colour to this characterful door decoration.

∗❋

⏱ *1 hour*

You will need:

∗ *evergreen twigs (such as pine)*
∗ *willow wreath*
∗ *wire*
∗ *small pine cones*
∗ *glue gun*
∗ *wool, here: red and pink*
∗ *card*
∗ *scissors*
∗ *moss*

∗ Tip ∗

When Christmas is over you can remove all the materials from the wreath, and either save them for next year, or redecorate the wreath at Easter.

To make this pretty wreath, you just need a willow wreath which you can adorn in a festive manner with colourful pompoms, twigs, and pine cones. As an added bonus, this is a great way of using up leftover bits of wool. It looks fantastic and all your visitors will immediately want their own.

How it's done:

1. Attach the twigs to the willow wreath using wire. Stick the cones in place using the glue gun. Add a touch of personality by making a couple of red and pink pompoms (see p121) in different sizes and use the glue gun again to attach these to the wreath.

2. Pick slender pieces of moss, wrap them round with wire and attach these little rolls to the wreath.

3. Finally, make two tassels (see p121) and hang them at different heights below the wreath.

①

Christmas tree decorations

Painted baubles

These pretty Christmas tree decorations are quick to make and far more attractive than many shop-bought trinkets.

You can buy ready-cut, natural wooden discs from craft supplies shops and then they just need to be painted. Adding a personal touch to this year's Christmas decorations is easier than you think.

How it's done:

1. First drill a little hole about 5mm (¼in) from the edge of each disc for hanging them later.

2. Now mix a bit of white acrylic paint with water to get a very thin consistency and glaze the wooden disc with it. The grain of the wood should remain visible, the colour is just a bit lighter. Let the glaze dry thoroughly.

3. Now you can paint both sides of the wooden disc in whatever way you fancy, using red paint or the silver marker pen. Use the star template to help you, or paint cheery Father Christmas faces or patterns on to the wooden discs. Once they are dry, pass the red thread through the holes to hang up your decorations.

✶✶❀

🕔 *5 minutes per decoration, plus drying time*

You will need:

* ✶ *drill and 3mm (⅛in) diameter drill bit*
* ✶ *wooden discs, 5–6cm (2–2½in) in diameter*
* ✶ *white and red acrylic paint*
* ✶ *thin flat paintbrush*
* ✶ *silver marker pen*
* ✶ *template (see p122)*
* ✶ *red thread*
* ✶ *scissors*

❷
Christmas tree decorations

Lebkuchen hearts

These are a classic German tradition and should be on every Christmas tree! Nibbling is positively encouraged.

＊＊❄
🕐 *2 hours, plus cooling time*

You will need:
For the biscuits:
* *150g (5½oz) honey*
* *75g (2½oz) caster sugar*
* *50g (1¾oz) unsalted butter*
* *1 tbsp cocoa powder*
* *50g (1¾oz) ground almonds*
* *1 tsp lebkuchen spices, from German stores or online*
* *1 small egg, lightly beaten*
* *pinch of salt*
* *275g (9½oz) plain flour*
* *2 tsp baking powder*

In addition:
* *baking tray*
* *baking parchment*
* *saucepan*
* *rolling pin*
* *heart-shaped cutter*
* *wide straw*
* *200g dark chocolate glaze, from German stores or online*
* *bain-marie*
* *handful of blanched almonds*
* *frying pan*
* *wire rack*
* *thin ribbon*

How it's done:

1. Preheat the oven to 200°C (400°F/Gas 6) and line a baking tray with baking parchment. Heat the honey, sugar, and butter in a saucepan until the sugar dissolves.

2. Leave the mixture to cool slightly, then stir in the cocoa, ground almonds, spices, egg, and salt. Next add the flour and baking powder and mix until you have a smooth dough.

3. Roll out the dough until it is about 5mm (¼in) thick and stamp out hearts. In the upper centre of each heart use a wide straw to punch a hole in the dough. Lay the hearts on the prepared tray and bake for 10–12 minutes, then leave to cool.

4. Heat the chocolate glaze over a bain-marie according to the packet instructions until it has melted.

5. Halve the almonds lengthways and toast them gently in a dry frying pan.

6. Put the hearts on a wire rack, coat with the glaze and press 2 almond halves into the glaze. As soon as the glaze has hardened, you can hang the hearts on your Christmas tree with thin ribbon.

*The custom of having a tree in your home and decorating
it at Christmas time has been around for hundreds of years.
The evergreen tree is a reminder of new life during the dark
winter months, while lit candles are a symbol of hope.*

Winter night dream-catcher

These atmospheric rings are a lovely idea for a gift, or for decorating bedrooms, especially children's rooms.

These are just right for this time of contemplation and help bring sweet dreams to overstimulated minds, particularly for children at Christmas! You can hang a little angel or other festive symbol inside the ring.

How it's done:

1. For the first ring, tweak a metal ring open with pliers. Now thread the wooden beads on to the ring and tie 4 short woollen strands between each. To do this, double the wool over, slip the loop under the ring, then take both yarn ends over the ring and through the loop. Next pull the loop firm and cut the wool ends to the same length. As soon as the ring has been completely adorned with beads and wool, close it again with a little piece of adhesive tape and push the decorations over the join.

2. For the second ring, knot the different coloured wools next to each other on the ring. You can tie them together, plait them, or hang beads on them. To finish off, you can hang a Christmas tree decoration inside the ring.

3. For the third ring, tie longer woollen strands on to the ring and use a yarn needle to thread beads on to them. End each string with a golden bead and secure it with a knot. The stepped shape is created by hanging either an extra bead or a bead less to each strand of wool as you progress along the ring.

✳ ❄ ❄

🕑 *30 minutes per ring*

You will need:
* ✳ *3 white metal rings: 1 x 15cm (6in) and 2 x 20cm (8in) in diameter*
* ✳ *universal pliers*
* ✳ *wooden beads, 1cm (½in) and 1.5cm (¾in) in diameter*
* ✳ *wool in shades of white, tan, and grey*
* ✳ *scissors*
* ✳ *adhesive tape*
* ✳ *Christmas tree decorations*
* ✳ *yarn needle*
* ✳ *golden glass beads, 5–10mm (¼–½in) in diameter*

"When you dream, you should set no limits"

Honoré de Balzac

Giving

Christmas means presents and, in our world, presents mean creativity. Home-made gifts are always special. In this chapter we will inspire you with a wealth of clever ideas that are both quick to make and guaranteed to bring joy to your loved ones.

Advent calendar

This lovely idea has a bag for every day of December up to Christmas Eve. It is destined to be a life-long companion; reused every year, or handed down to younger siblings.

Use a stamp to print little motifs on the individual Advent calendar pouches, which you can then hang up where you choose. This delightful calendar is easy to make and offers enough room for 24 little treats and presents. And, once Christmas is over, you can store it away in a pretty bag for next year.

How it's done:

1. First cut out the copied templates.

2. Now transfer the shapes and numbers on to the foam and cut them all out.

3. Stick the motif on the outside of a transparent CD case. (After stamping you can peel it off again and stick on another one, so you don't need a new CD case for every motif.)

4. Use a little sponge to dab some fabric dye of your choice on to the foam until the entire surface is evenly covered. ➥

★ ❋ ❋
⏱ *3–4 hours*

You will need:

* *templates (see pp123–125)*
* *pen*
* *scissors*
* *self-adhesive foam*
* *old CD cases*
* *little sponges*
* *fabric dye in red, blue, yellow, and green*
* *newspaper*
* *12 cotton bags, about 15 × 10cm (6 × 4in)*
* *12 cotton bags, about 20 × 15cm (8 × 6in)*
* *iron*
* *needle and thread*
* *24 bells*
* *1 large fabric bag, about 40 × 30cm (16 × 12in)*

5. Lay some newspaper inside the cotton bags to stop the dye coming through both layers, then stamp the foam shape on to the material. On the back of the bag stamp one of the numbers between 1 and 24.

6. Allow the fabric dye to dry and then fix it according to the packet instructions, with the iron.

7. Finally, sew a bell on to each of the bottom corners of the large cotton bags.

8. On the large fabric bag you can print the name of the future owner, plus various motifs. This bag can be used to store the Advent calendar between Christmases.

* Tip *

Stamp different motifs one after another with the same colour, so you don't need to wash out the sponge every time.

🎁

***The origins of the Advent calendar can be traced back to the 19th century.
The first Advent calendars consisted of 24 little pictures with Christmas
designs, which would be hung up individually on each day. Alternatively,
people simply drew 24 chalk marks on the wall, one of which was wiped
away each day, to show how many days were left until Christmas.***

Good luck angel

Not only is this angel really attractive, it also has a very special place at Christmas.

From its position at the window, or on a door, it listens closely to what the people who live in the home want for Christmas, and also protects the family from conflict and upset during the festive season.

How it's done:

1. Fold the red craft felt in half widthways, lay the cut-out template on it and trace the outline. The straight edge should be lined up flush with the folded-over edge of the fabric. Then cut out the angel.

2. Sew up the sides using buttonhole stitch (see p107) leaving an opening of about 5cm (2in), then stuff the angel with the wadding. Finally, sew up the opening.

** ** ❋

🕐 *1–2 hours*

You will need:

* *A4 sheets of craft felt in red and pink*
* *templates (see p126)*
* *pen*
* *scissors*
* *needle*
* *red and gold thread*
* *wadding material*
* *2mm (⅛in) beads in pale blue, pink, and yellow*
* *various larger beads*
* *golden bell*

3. Cut out the crown from the pink felt and sew it to the head using running stitch (see p108). Decorate the crown and robe with beads. Sew tassels (see p121) made from gold thread on to the corners of the skirt.

4. Finally, thread a short string of beads and the bell and sew it centrally to the bottom edge of the angel. Attach a thin thread to the angel's head to hang it up.

Soap diamonds

This DIY project isn't just for Christmas: if you make enough, it should provide a wonderfully fragrant reminder of your gift all year round.

* ❄ ❄

🕐 *15 minutes, plus drying time*

You will need:

* *large saucepan*
* *small saucepan, or heatproof bowl*
* *raw soap, transparent and white*
* *diamond-shaped silicone mould*

These little crystal-shaped soaps are quick to make and can be enriched with various scents, or combined with herb leaves and flower petals.

How it's done:

1. Heat some water in a large saucepan. Then suspend a smaller saucepan, or heatproof bowl, over the larger one, add the raw soap and melt it in this bain-marie.

2. When the raw soap has completely melted, pour it into a silicone mould and put it in a cool place. After about 1 hour the soap will have solidified and you can release the individual pieces from the mould.

"A true gift is something you offer to someone else that you would rather have kept for yourself"

Selma Lagerlöf

* Tip *

You can add fragrance to the soap by using an essential oil of your choice. Just add a couple of drops of oil to the liquid soap before you pour it into the mould.

❶
Cosmetic bags
Striped bag

This is a lovely gift for anyone who needs to stash their toiletries safely when traveling. Tips and tricks for knitting can be found from page 110.

How it's done:

1. The bag is knitted completely in garter stitch (see p112). Loosely cast on 27 stitches in blue.

2. Work the 1st row in blue, then 2 rows in white (with yarn doubled), then 2 rows in blue.

3. Continue in these alternating colours. Finish when the piece measures about 25cm (10in) ending on a blue row, and cast off loosely on the reverse side. The knitted piece should measure about 26 × 20cm (10 × 8in).

4. Fold the knitted piece in half with the wrong side facing outwards. Sew up the side seams and sew in all the loose ends.

5. Turn the bag the right way out. The pouch should now measure about 20 × 13cm (8 × 5in).

6. Finally, prepare and insert the bag lining and zip (see p49).

"The more we make other people happy, the more joy we receive in our own heart in return"

Traditional proverb

✳✳✳
🕐 *3–4 hours*

You will need:
For the knitted bag:
* *50cm (20in) 7mm (UK size 2) circular needle*
* *about 30g (1oz) blue wool, here: Lamana Nazca (40% alpaca, 40% merino, 20% nylon)*
* *about 30g (1oz) white wool, here: Lamana Cusco (100% alpaca), knitted with the wool held double*
* *1 yarn needle*
* *scissors*

For the lining:
* *35 × 25cm (14 × 10in) fabric*
* *blue thread*
* *18cm (7in) long colourful zip*
* *needle*
* *pins*
* *sewing machine*

❷

Cosmetic bags

Two-tone bag

Whether for cosmetics, pens, or loose change, this pretty woollen bag is a must.

How it's done:

1. Loosely cast on 27 stitches in white (with the yarn held double).

2. Knit 6 rows in moss stitch (see p114).

3. On the 7th row, knit 2, then, from the doubled yarn, knit 1 stitch from the first strand and another stitch from the second strand (so 2 knit stitches are created from a single stitch), then continue with knit 1, knit 2 stitches from 1, knit 1, knit 2 stitches from 1, to the end of the row, finishing with an edge stitch. (39 stitches)

4. Switch to anthracite: knit 1 stitch, purl to the last stitch, then knit the last stitch. Continue in stocking stitch.

5. When the piece measures about 21cm (8½in), switch to white on a right side row: knit 1, *1 knit stitch, knit 2 together, repeat from * to the last 2 stitches, then knit 2. (27 stitches)

6. Then work a further 6 rows in moss stitch and cast off loosely on row 7.

7. Measure your knitted piece. The white upper and lower edges should be about 21cm (8½in) wide, the middle section in anthracite about 29cm (11½in) wide. Thanks to the increases and decreases at the colour transition, the knitted piece is convex in shape. You will need to take this into account when cutting the lining fabric to size.

8. Fold the knitting in half with the wrong side facing out. Sew up the side seams and sew in all the loose ends.

9. Turn the bag right way out. The pouch should now be about 29cm (11½in) wide at the bottom, 21cm (8½in) wide at the top and about 14cm (5½in) tall. To prepare and insert the lining fabric, see opposite.

✳✳✳

⏱ *3–4 hours*

You will need:

For the knitted bag:

* *50cm (20in) 7mm (UK size 2) circular needle*
* *about 30g (1oz) white wool, here: Lamana Cusco (100% alpaca), knitted with the wool held double*
* *about 60g (2oz) anthracite colour wool, here: Lamana Nazca (40% alpaca, 40% merino, 20% nylon)*
* *1 yarn needle*
* *scissors*

For the lining:

* *paper pattern (see p127)*
* *35 × 35cm (14 × 14in) fabric*
* *18cm (7in) long colourful zip*
* *pins*
* *sewing machine*
* *needle*
* *white thread*

Lining bag and finishing
How it's done:

The same approach is used for both designs.

1. For the striped bag, cut the fabric according to the dimensions of the knitted pouch, adding 1cm (½in) seam allowance at the sides. For the two-tone bag, use the template (see p127), and this time add a 2cm (¾in) seam allowance.

2. Pin the zip on to the right side of the material along the short edge (the zip pull should be on top) and sew the upper zip tape in place with a sewing machine. Pin and sew the other edge in a similar manner.

3. Now sew up the side seams (using the seam allowance of 1cm / ½in), from the bottom up to the zip seam.

4. Place the lining bag inside the knitted bag. Pin the upper edges together, taking care that the side seams are aligned.

5. Hand-sew the knitted bag to the zip fastener, using the needle and thread and making small adjustments as you go to avoid bunching.

Family t-shirts

Over Christmas not only are you allowed to slow down, but some proper rest and recuperation – including pottering about in comfortable clothes – are positively encouraged.

With this in mind, we have designed comfy handmade outfits for the whole family, so you can look good (and festive) while you're having a lie-in.

How it's done:

1. The t-shirts are all printed with the same design. We've varied the colours a bit. First, cut out the copied templates, transfer them to the foam, and cut them all out. Stick the foam motifs on to the outside of a transparent CD case.

2. Use the little sponge to dab a bit of your chosen fabric dye on to the foam until the entire surface is evenly covered.

3. Lay some newspaper inside the t-shirts to stop the dye from penetrating both layers, then stamp on the foam shapes. Leave the fabric dye to dry and then fix it according to the packet instructions, with the iron.

4. For the kid's t-shirt we used a cotton bud to print red dots on to a Christmas tree, and also painted a smiling face on the tree.

✳ ❄ ❄

🕘 *15 minutes per shirt*

You will need:

✳ *templates (see p128)*
✳ *pen*
✳ *scissors*
✳ *self-adhesive foam*
✳ *old CD cases*
✳ *little sponge*
✳ *fabric dye in green, white, black, red, and yellow*
✳ *newspaper*
✳ *white t-shirts for the whole family*
✳ *iron*
✳ *cotton buds*

✳ Tip ✳

If you prefer, design your own family Christmas motif and use that instead of our template.

Photo cube

Great for your shelves or bedside table.

You will need:

∗ *cutter*
∗ *cutting board*
∗ *ruler with a steel edge*
∗ *printed-out photos*
∗ *glue stick*
∗ *paper to use as underlay*
∗ *2 wooden cubes, 7cm (3in) and 10cm (4in)*

Shared memories are something to treasure. That's why this photo cube is the ideal present for close friends, family, or your partner. It doesn't take long to make and it is something really personal; so much more original and versatile than a traditional picture frame.

How it's done:

1. Cut your photos to shape. For our 7cm (3in) and 10cm (4in) cubes we cut our pictures to measure 6cm² (2½in²) and 9cm² (3½in²).

2. Apply glue evenly over the back of the photos, laying some paper underneath to prevent your work surface from getting dirty.

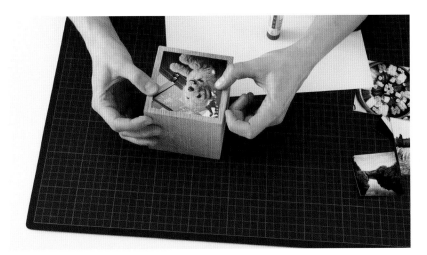

3. Now stick the photos centrally on each side of the wooden cube.

❶
Cuddly star
Large crochet star

*These adorable stars are designed as a gift for younger kids.
They are perfect travel companions, or make a little friend
for cuddling in bed.*

How it's done:

Both stars are made in 2 sections using double crochet stitch. First you crochet from the centre out in a spiral (which creates a slightly bulging shape), then you crochet the points of the star back and forth in rows. Tips and tricks for crocheting can be found from page 116.

1st round: crochet a 5 stitch loop.
2nd round: double crochet into every stitch. (10 stitches)
3rd round: double crochet into every 2nd stitch. (15 stitches)
4th round: double crochet into every 3rd stitch. (20 stitches)
5th round: double crochet into every 4th stitch. (25 stitches)
6th round: double crochet into every 5th stitch. (30 stitches)
7th round: double crochet into every 6th stitch. (35 stitches)
8th round: double crochet into every 7th stitch. (40 stitches)
9th round: double crochet into every 8th stitch. (45 stitches)
10th round: double crochet into every 9th stitch. (50 stitches)
11th round: double crochet into every 10th stitch. (55 stitches)
12th round: double crochet into every 11th stitch. (60 stitches)
13th round: double crochet into every 12th stitch. (65 stitches)
14th round: double crochet into every 13th stitch. (70 stitches)

Now you crochet the 5 points of the star in rows as follows (as you have 70 stiches, there will be 14 stitches for each point of the star):

1. For the 1st point of the star, double crochet 14 stitches (insert a stitch marker in the following stitch – this is where you will later start the 2nd point). Turn the work.

2. Next row: no turning chain stitch, skip 1 stitch, double crochet to the end of the row. Continue in this manner, decreasing 1 stitch per row, and the point will form nice and evenly. Finally you are left with 1 stitch. Cut the thread and pull it through the loop. ➥

∗∗∗
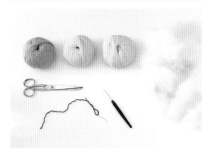
🕑 *2–3 hours*

You will need:

∗ *4.5mm (UK 7: US 7) crochet hook*
∗ *about 100g (3½oz) wool in grey or white, here: Lamana Cusco (100% alpaca)*
∗ *stitch marker*
∗ *scissors*
∗ *yarn needle*
∗ *about 30g (1oz) wadding material*
∗ *embroidery needle (optional)*
∗ *black wool scraps (optional)*

Finished dimensions: about 24cm (9½in) in diameter

3. The 2nd point begins from the stitch marker. Remove the stitch marker, join in the yarn again here and crochet a chain stitch (this counts as the first stitch). Double crochet a further 13 stitches up to the end of the row, turn the work and crochet this point exactly as you did for the first. Work the remaining points in the same way.

4. Crochet the second side of the star as above.

5. Carefully sew up any loose threads on the wrong side (the interior) of both sections. Firmly pull the thread from the loop at the start and likewise sew in this end.

6. Lay the 2 sections with wrong sides facing and double crochet the edges of the points together. At the upper end of the points, double crochet 3 times into 1 stitch.

7. When only 2 edges are open, start stuffing in the wadding material: take small quantities of the wadding and use the handle of your crochet hook to push these into the points of each star. Continue filling to the centre making sure this is particularly well stuffed.

8. For the 2 final edges you will have to alternate between crocheting the seam together and inserting more wadding. Cut the final thread and secure it well. Mould the star into shape. If you like, you can embroider a face with black wool.

"It is Christmas in the heart that puts Christmas in the air"

William Turner Ellis

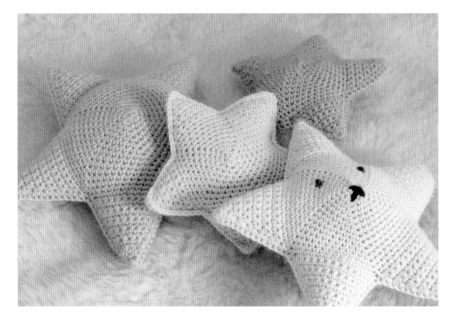

Cuddly star

Small crochet star

This smaller variant of the same star is an even cuter present for cuddling and playing.

How it's done:

1. Work the small star up to and including the 10th row in exactly the same way as for the large star. After the 10th round there are 50 stitches. Now the 5 points are crocheted in rows as follows (as you have 50 stiches, there will be 10 stitches for each point of the star):

2. For the 1st point, double crochet 10 stitches (insert a stitch marker in the next stitch; this is where you will later begin the 2nd point). Turn the work.

3. Next row: no turning chain stitch, skip 1 stitch, double crochet to the end of the row. Continue in this way, crocheting the first point as described for the large star.

4. The 2nd point begins from the stitch marker. Remove the stitch marker, join in the yarn again, and crochet a chain stitch (this counts as the first stitch). Double crochet a further 9 stitches to the end of the row, turn the work, and crochet as described above to the end.

5. Work the remaining points and the second half of the star as described for the large star. Similarly, crochet the 2 halves together and stuff the star.

✻✻✻
🕑 *2–3 hours*

You will need:
* *4.5mm (UK 7: US 7) crochet hook*
* *about 50g (1¾oz) pale blue or yellow wool: here Lamana Cusco (100% alpaca)*
* *stitch marker*
* *scissors*
* *yarn needle*
* *about 20g (¾oz) wadding material*

Finished dimensions: about 18cm (7in) in diameter

✻ Tip ✻

To help count your spiral rounds, mark the first stitch of each new round with a stitch marker.

Caramel hearts

Christmas is the best time to indulge your sweet tooth. If someone you love is a fan of sweet hot drinks, these sugar hearts are perfect.

Just add them to hot milk, coffee, or tea and enjoy! The ideal gift to take to a holiday gathering.

How it's done:

1. Warm the sugar in a saucepan over a medium heat until it melts. Don't put it over a high heat, or take your eyes off the pan, because the caramelized sugar burns easily. Children's hands have no business here.

2. When the caramel is light golden in colour, remove the saucepan from the heat. Stir some cinnamon into the liquid caramel to give it a Christmassy flavour, if you like, but it also tastes great without this addition.

3. Pour the liquid mixture into the silicone mould and leave to cool. Do not touch hot caramel, however tempted you may be to have a taste!

∗ ❄ ❄
🕙 *30 minutes*

You will need:

∗ *500g (1lb 2oz) white granulated sugar (see below)*
∗ *saucepan*
∗ *1 tsp ground cinnamon, or to taste (optional)*
∗ *silicone heart mould*

∗ Tip ∗

It is vital to use white sugar here. Brown or golden sugars won't caramelize.

Typography picture

Letters have long since been an interior design winner,
and who would guess it's so easy to produce your own fantastic,
customized typography design?

∗ ∗ ❊

🕑 *about 1 hour per picture*

You will need:

∗ *graphite paper*
∗ *birch plywood panels, 10–15mm*
  (½–¾in) thick, 50 × 25cm
  (20 × 10in) and 20 × 20cm
  (8 × 8in)
∗ *templates (see p129)*
∗ *adhesive tape*
∗ *ballpoint pen*
∗ *black and anthracite acrylic paint*
∗ *flat paintbrush, 2cm (¾in) wide*
∗ *thin round paintbrush*

This monochrome look is not only totally on trend, it also works really well in most homes, but you can use colours if you prefer.

How it's done:

1. Lay the graphite paper with the coated side facing down on to a wooden panel. Place the template centrally on top and fix it in place with the adhesive tape.

2. Trace the contour of the typographical template with a ballpoint pen to copy the motif on to the panel.

3. Now remove the template and paper and paint the wood with acrylic paint, either painting the letter or the area around it. Use a flat brush for large areas and a thin round brush for the finer work around the corners and edges.

Kitchen apron

A great gift for the person making Christmas dinner, or even for the reluctant cook who you want to get involved in the kitchen.

There's no reason why an apron shouldn't also look stylish. This is a lovely present for anyone who likes to spend time in the kitchen cooking, baking, or simply pottering about. And it's a simple sewing project for beginners.

How it's done:

1. Fold the fabric in half lengthways, with right sides facing, and lay the pattern along the fold. Pin the template in place on the fabric and trace the outline using tailor's chalk or pencil. Cut out the apron and all 3 straps.

2. First sew the straps. To do this, fold in both the long edges, fix with pins, and stitch along both sides.

3. Now hem the apron. Fold the outer edge over twice by 1cm (½in), pin in place, and stitch. This works best if you start with the 2 arm sections (seam A on the template), then stitch along the sides (B), and finally the lower edge of the apron. ➤➤

✳✳❊

🕙 *1–2 hours*

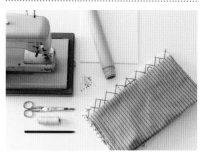

You will need:

✳ *cotton fabric, 140 × 100cm (4.5ft × 3ft 3in)*
✳ *pattern template (see p130)*
✳ *pins*
✳ *tailor's chalk, or pencil*
✳ *scissors*
✳ *sewing machine*
✳ *cotton thread*

For sewing tips and tricks, see p107.

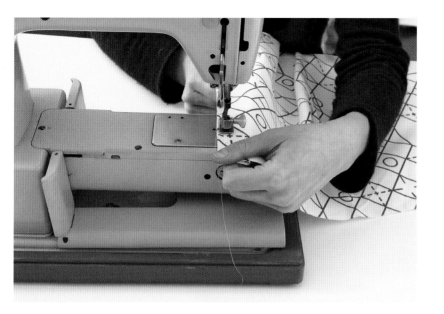

4. After this, sew the straps on to the apron: first fold the open end of the long straps inwards and stitch. Then pin the straps on the reverse side of the apron at position F, and sew them on from the right side.

5. Fold over the top edge (C) twice, as you did before; the turnover here should be 3.5cm (1½in) wide.

6. Now you sew the neck strap on to the apron. Lay both ends of the loop which will go around the head under the turnover (G). Stitch the lower seam (D) of the turnover, fixing the neck loop in place as you do this. Finally fold up the neck loop and stitch the upper seam (E). This stitches the neck strap firmly in place for a second time.

"Give sincerely and freely. Bestow what dwells within you – your opinions, taste, and humour – and you will be abundantly rewarded"

Joachim Ringelnatz

* Tip *

To make the hemming easier here, iron all the edges and pin them in place before sewing.

Crunchy coffee-break biscuits

Been invited to a festive coffee morning? Why not take along something you've baked?

These beautifully decorated biscuits are not just delicious, they are also the perfect decorative gift for tea and coffee lovers.

How it's done:

1. Preheat the oven to 180°C (350°F/Gas 4). Line a baking tray with baking parchment.

2. Put the flour, butter, sugar, egg, baking powder, vanilla, cocoa, and salt into a large bowl and knead together until you have a smooth dough.

3. Shape little balls from the dough, each slightly smaller than a walnut, then roll these between your hands to create a little roll. Bend the dough rolls into a U-shape and press the underside flat on to the work surface. Lay the biscuits on the prepared tray and bake for about 10 minutes until crisp. Leave to cool.

4. Now shape little rolls out of the fondant icing, bend them into a U-shape and flatten the base, then press them on to the flat underside of the biscuits. Press chopped pistachios into the icing.

∗∗❄

🕐 *2 hours, plus cooling time*

You will need:
For the biscuits:
* *250g (9oz) plain flour*
* *125g (4½oz) unsalted butter, softened*
* *90g (3oz) caster sugar*
* *1 egg, lightly beaten*
* *¼ tsp baking powder*
* *½ tsp vanilla extract*
* *1 tsp cocoa powder*
* *pinch of salt*
* *100g (3½oz) white fondant icing*
* *25g (½oz) chopped pistachios*

In addition:
* *baking tray*
* *baking parchment*

Beaded jumper

There's no need to wear a necklace if your clothing is gently sparkling with translucent pearly beads.

∗ ❋ ❋

🕓 *1 hour*

You will need:

∗ *beading needle*
∗ *thread in a suitable colour*
∗ *glass wax beads, 4mm (¼in) diameter*
∗ *woollen jumper*
∗ *scissors*

With just a few stitches you can jazz up a simple jumper in festive fashion. Simply stitch on a few pretty beads and your Christmas top is ready: a really special present.

How it's done:

1. Using a beading needle and thread, sew pearly beads on to the jumper. Take care to sew in the loose thread ends. If the beads are spaced no further than 3–4cm (1¼–1½in) apart, you can run the thread between them on the inside of the garment.

2. You can arrange the beads spaced out exactly as you please. We began at the top with lots of beads, then gradually spaced them out more widely further down. We left the sleeves completely plain, but of course the beads look absolutely lovely there, too, if you prefer.

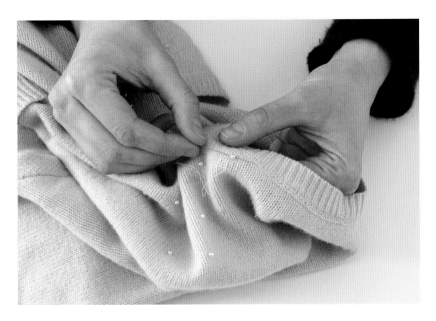

Knitted slippers

***Slippers are a thoughtful and welcome gift, hugging the feet of
your loved ones and keeping them cosy and warm.***

Our knitted slippers are comfortable to wear, and also look great. For small
and large feet, to give away, or keep for yourself! You will find tips and tricks
on knitting from page 110.

How it's done:

Tension sample: 17 stitches and 22 rows stocking stitch, with the yarn knitted
double, using 5mm (UK size 6) needles = 10 × 10cm (4 × 4in).

The slippers are knitted with the yarn held double. If you have 2 balls of wool,
knit with a strand from each ball. If you only have 1 ball, find the end of the
yarn in the centre of the ball and knit this together with the thread coming
from the outside.

Both slippers are knitted identically, partly in stocking stitch, partly in
garter stitch. Initially they are knitted back and forth, then in rounds on the
double-pointed needles. For the garter stitch selvedge, the edge stitches are
worked by slipping the first stitch knit-wise at the start of each row; the final
stitch in each row is simply knitted. The details for the different sizes are
given in brackets: size 1 (size 2: size 3: size 4: size 5).➻

∗∗∗

🕑 *1–4 hours per pair, depending
on size and knitting ability*

You will need:

∗ *set of 20cm (8in) long 5mm
(UK 6: US 8) double-pointed needles*
∗ *wool in 2 colours, here: Lamana
Cusco (100% alpaca), quantity
according to size:*
 Size 1
 *(27–29, 4–6 years, foot length about
17.5cm / 7in): about 50g (1¾oz)
colour A, about 15g (½oz) colour B*
 Size 2
 *(30–32, 7–9 years, foot length about
19.5cm / 7¾in): about 100g (3½oz)
colour A, about 30g (1oz) colour B*
 Size 3
 *(35–36, foot length about 22cm /
8¾in): about 100g (3½oz) colour A,
about 30g (1oz) colour B*
 Size 4
 *(38–39, foot length about 24cm /
9½in): about 100g (3½oz) colour A,
about 30g (1oz) colour B*
 Size 5
 *(40–41, foot length about 26cm /
10½in): about 130g (4¾oz) colour
A, about 45g (1½oz) colour B*
∗ *stitch marker*
∗ *scissors*
∗ *yarn needle*

1. Cast on 26 (30:30:34:38) stitches loosely in colour A with the yarn held double. The trailing yarn end should be about 25cm (10in) long, to allow you to use this to sew up the heel seam later.

2. 1st row (wrong side): edge stitch, knit 4 (5:5:6:6), purl 16 (18:18:20:24), knit 4 (5:5:6:6), edge stitch.

3. 2nd row (right side): edge stitch, knit to end, edge stitch.

4. Repeat the 1st and 2nd rows until, after about 20 (22:26:28:30) rows, the piece measures 8 (9:11.5:12.5:13.5) cm (3 [3½:4½:5:5¼] in).

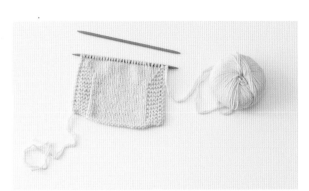

5. From the next wrong side row, reduce the lateral garter stitch sections on every wrong side row as follows: edge stitch, knit 3 (4:4:5:5), purl 18 (20:20:22:26), knit 3 (4:4:5:5), edge stitch.

6. Next right side row: edge stitch, knit to end, edge stitch.

7. Next wrong side row: edge stitch, knit 2 (3:3:4:4), purl 20 (22:22:24:28), knit 2 (3:3:4:4), edge stitch.

8. Next right side row: edge stitch, knit to end, edge stitch.

9. Reduce the garter stitch section in this manner until on a wrong side row there is just 1 stitch knitted

between the edge stitches at the start and end of the row, and the stitches in between are all purl stitches. The piece should measure 11 (12.5:14:16:17.5) cm (4¼ [5:5½:6¼:7] in) and have 25 (29:33:37:39) rows.

10. On the next right side row, the stitches are distributed between 4 double-pointed needles. The 1st needle is always the beginning of a round. To help you count the rounds, place a stitch marker on needle 1. On needle 1, work the 1st decrease: knit 1, SKP (slip one (knitwise), knit 1, pass slipped stitch over). On needle 4, work the 2nd decrease: knit the second- and third-last stitches on the needle together. There should now be 6 (7:7:8:9) stitches on each needle.

11. On the 4th round (counting from the stitch marker on needle 1), switch to colour B at the start of the 3rd needle. Cut the double strands of colour A and continue to knit in rounds.

12. At the start of round 5 (5:5:6:6) in colour B, begin decreasing for the tip (start on needle 1). To do this, work the 1st decrease on needles 1 and 3 and the 2nd decrease on needles 2 and 4. Work the decreases on every other round until there are 5 (4:4:5:5) stitches on every needle.

13. Now work the decreases on every round until there are 2 stitches on each needle for any size of slipper. Cut the double strands and use a yarn needle to pull these through the remaining stitches.

14. Turn the slipper wrong side out and sew in the threads carefully on the inside at the tip and at the colour change.

15. Fold over the cast on edge (at the rear centre) and close the heel seam neatly, using the wool you left hanging from when you cast on. Work the second slipper in exactly the same way.

"That which issues from the heart alone,
will bend the hearts of others to your own"

Johann Wolfgang von Goethe

Wrapping

Beautifully wrapped gifts are not just fun to receive, but preparing them also adds to the excited anticipation of Christmas Day. The projects in this chapter show that original gift-wrapping ideas don't have to be a lot of work.

Festive gift wrap with paper bows

Creative gifts with a thoughtful and personal touch of detail are a particular joy to receive; at Christmas the wrapping paper is far more than just packaging.

Really special wrapping ideas don't have to involve lots of time or money. With just a few small steps and a bit of creativity, you can transform your presents into something so beautiful that no one will want to unwrap them!

How it's done:

1. Use a calligraphy pen to transform your handwriting and create a gift wrap design. Write out festive texts, such as poems or lyrics, in generously curved letters on the plain wrapping paper.

2. To make the pretty bow, use the template to cut both sections out of white paper. Dab a bit of glue in the centre of section A and press both ends firmly on top. Then glue this bow centrally on to section B.

✱ ❀ ❀

🕑 *15 minutes*

You will need:

✱ *calligraphy pen*
✱ *plain wrapping paper*
✱ *bow template (see p131)*
✱ *scissors*
✱ *white paper*
✱ *glue stick*

Ribbons

*These pretty fabric ribbons add a home-made touch to any
gift wrap, and they are quick and easy to make yourself
from recycled fabric remnants.*

* ❀ ❀

🕑 *5 minutes per ribbon,
plus drying time*

You will need:

* *thin white cotton fabric*
* *scissors*
* *foil or paper to use as underlay*
* *wide flat paintbrush*
* *silk paint in blue, pink, and green*
* *small drinking glass*
* *iron*

We tore fabric into long strips, then dyed it with silk paint to upcycle
it into gift wrap ribbon.

How it's done:

1. Rip the cotton fabric into narrow strips. To do this, snip slightly into the material following the direction of the fabric grain, then tear down from this incision. You will get lovely evenly frayed edges.

2. Lay the fabric strips on your underlay and brush with water.

3. Dilute some silk paint with water in a small drinking glass, then brush the wet fabric strip with this so it has an even colour.

4. Leave the fabric strip to dry, then fix the colour with the iron, according to the silk dye packet instructions.

Biscuit gift tags

Have you got a horde of kids, great-grandmas, second cousins, and adopted "family" coming for Christmas this year? To avoid any mix-ups when the presents are handed out, the best idea is to attach little name tags to each.

These biscuit tags are easy to bake and can be gobbled up as soon as the presents have been distributed.

How it's done:

1. Preheat the oven to 220°C (425°F/Gas 7). Line a baking tray with baking parchment. In a large bowl, mix the flour, blancmange powder, baking powder, sugar, ground almonds, salt, cinnamon, ginger, and vanilla.

2. Brown the butter in a small saucepan, then let it cool slightly.

3. Now add the butter, honey, and eggs to the bowl of dry ingredients and work everything together until you have a smooth, firm dough. Leave the dough to rest for 15 minutes in the fridge.

4. Dust a work surface with flour and roll the dough out thinly using a rolling pin. Stamp out individual biscuits and use the letter stamp to print names in the biscuits. Make a little hole in the dough at the top of each using a straw.

5. Place the biscuits on the prepared baking tray. Bake for around 10 minutes until they are golden brown, then leave to cool.

6. Finally, melt the chocolate glaze over a bain-marie according to the manufacturer's instructions. Once it has completely melted, dip the lower half of each biscuit into the chocolate. Let the chocolate coating solidify. You can attach the biscuits to the presents using a little ribbon through the hole.

◂◂ *The paper gift tags can be found at the back of the book!*

✷✷❊
🕐 *2 hours, plus cooling time*

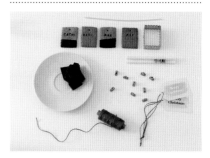

You will need:
For the biscuits:
* *300g (10oz) plain flour*
* *1 sachet of chocolate blancmange*
* *2 tsp baking powder*
* *150g (5½oz) caster sugar*
* *75g (2½oz) ground almonds*
* *pinch of salt*
* *pinch of ground cinnamon*
* *1 tsp ground ginger*
* *1 tsp vanilla extract*
* *150g (5½oz) unsalted butter*
* *1 tbsp runny honey*
* *2 eggs, lightly beaten*

In addition:
* *cookie cutters*
* *letter stamps*
* *straw*
* *200g dark chocolate glaze, from German stores or online*
* *bain-marie*
* *thin ribbon*

Envelopes for Christmas post

Wherever your loved ones might be, Christmas is a chance to surprise them with a few handwritten words.

∗ ❄ ❄

🕐 *2 minutes per envelope*

You will need:

∗ *self-adhesive address labels*
∗ *coloured envelopes*
∗ *glue stick*
∗ *copper-coloured glitter*

∗ Tip ∗

If the labels stick on too strongly and won't come off the envelopes, stick them on to a piece of fabric briefly beforehand. They will pick up little textile fibres which then prevent the label from sticking too firmly.

After all, it's always lovely to get real post, especially in this age of email. This project shows you how to design a special envelope to suit the occasion for your Christmas missive.

How it's done:

1. First stick an address label on a coloured envelope in the position where the address will go later.

2. Use a glue stick to mark round the label, applying the glue evenly, so the glitter will adhere.

3. Now scatter some glitter on to the sticky surface, spreading it with your finger and pressing slightly. Shake the loose glitter off over the sink.

4. Finally, you just need to pull off the address label carefully, to leave a clear, well-defined space in which to address the letter.

Rudolph gift wrap

Who's that peeking out at us? Rudolph! The friendly
face with the famous red nose will particularly thrill
young kids. This is a fun idea for a craft activity to brighten
up the pre-Christmas period, too.

How it's done:

1. First wrap up your present in the brown wrapping paper. Copy the antler templates with a colour photocopier and cut them out (or just make them out of brown paper).

2. To make the eyes, punch out a couple of circles from black paper using a hole punch. Stick them on using the glue stick. You could also cut out eyes by hand, or paint them.

✱ ❈ ❈
🕒 *5 minutes per present*

You will need:

* ✱ *brown wrapping paper*
* ✱ *templates (see pp132–33)*
* ✱ *scissors*
* ✱ *black paper*
* ✱ *hole punch*
* ✱ *glue stick*
* ✱ *1 red pompom per present,*
  1–2cm (½–¾in) in diameter
* ✱ *scalpel or craft knife*

3. Below the eyes, stick on the pompom as the nose. Use the scalpel to make a little slit in the gift wrap along the front edge where the antlers should go.

4. Fold over the ends of the antlers by about 1cm (½in), dab a bit of glue on to both sides of the folded-over ends, stick them into the slit in the paper, and press them into place.

Gift bags

A lovely packaging idea to wrap small presents for colleagues, friends at school, the postman, and all those other lovely people whose Christmas you want to brighten up a little.

✱✱❄

🕐 *15 minutes to make the transfer,*
   2 minutes for printing each bag

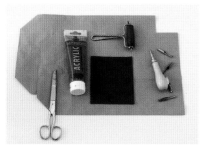

You will need:

∗ *scissors*
∗ *template (see pp134–135)*
∗ *linoleum sheet*
∗ *pencil*
∗ *linoleum cutters*
∗ *acrylic paint*
∗ *card*
∗ *linoleum ink roller (brayer)*
∗ *paper bags*

How it's done:

1. Cut out the template and transfer the shape on to the linoleum using the pencil. Use the linoleum cutter to carve out the lines which shouldn't be printed (these are printed black on the template). Take care when using the cutting tool to work away from your body, moving the linoleum rather than the tool, so you don't cut yourself. Finally, cut out the heart shape itself.

2. Put some acrylic paint on to a piece of card. Roll out the paint with the ink roller until the roller is coated. When the roller is evenly covered with paint, transfer the paint on to the linoleum heart.

3. As soon as the linoleum has been evenly covered in the paint, print the shape on to a paper bag.

Money crackers

At first sight, giving money might not seem particularly creative, but this wrapping makes each note bespoke.

These DIY Christmas crackers can be individually designed and are a lot prettier than an envelope. You can also fill the crackers with confetti, lucky charms, or home-made mottos for a New Year's Eve party.

How it's done:

⁎ ❋ ❋
🕑 *5 minutes per cracker*

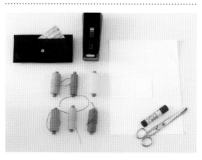

You will need:
* ⁎ *sheets of thick paper,*
  14 × 6.5cm (5½ × 2½in)
* ⁎ *adhesive tape*
* ⁎ *glue stick*
* ⁎ *1 A4 sheet of white tissue*
  paper per cracker
* ⁎ *bank notes, or other cracker contents*
* ⁎ *colourful thread*
* ⁎ *scissors*

1. Shape 1 of the thick pieces of paper into a little tube with a diameter of roughly 3cm (1¼in). Fix the tube in place using a piece of tape, then stuff the bank note inside.

2. Spread some glue along one side of this paper tube.

3. Lay the paper tube along a short end of the tissue paper sheet so that it sticks in place. Now roll up the paper tube inside the tissue paper, and glue the edge in place.

4. Tie up the cracker on both sides with the coloured thread. Finally, cut both ends of the cracker so they are the same length.

Wenn wir um Träume ...
alle unendlich sind,
uns alle Kinder führen
wie es sein soll, wie ...
Joachim Ringelnatz

Gift voucher baubles

If you want to give someone a gift voucher, these transparent baubles are a particularly pretty way to present them.

The baubles can be stuffed with a personal message or seasonal quotation, then hung on the tree until the moment that presents are handed out and they give up their secrets.

How it's done:

1. Cut the paper to an appropriate size for your bauble. Our baubles measure 7.5cm (3in) in diameter, so we cut our gift voucher slips to roughly 8 × 5cm (3 × 2in). Write your message on the paper.

2. Carefully remove the hanging mount from the bauble, roll up the paper with the writing facing outwards, and insert this into the bauble so it can be read through the ornament.

✽ ❋ ❋
🕙 *10 minutes per bauble*

You will need:

✽ *scissors*
✽ *paper*
✽ *pen, ideally a calligraphy pen*
✽ *transparent Christmas tree bauble with detachable hanging mount*

3. Replace the hanging mount… and you're done.

✽ Tip ✽

If the gift voucher is too big it will either not fit in the bauble at all, or it won't unfurl. It should be legible when it is inside the bauble.

Last-minute ideas

Has Christmas suddenly crept up on you
this year? No problem! With these quick ideas,
you can conjure up something festive
in no time at all.

Decorating

Candle bottles

These beautiful candlesticks bring a festive mood to your home, and can be made in just a few minutes.

Long candles take centre stage with the help of a couple of pretty, aromatic sprigs from different types of evergreen and some decorative glass bottles. What's more, your house will have a beautiful woodland and wintry scent. A great idea for rapidly conjuring up a Christmassy atmosphere.

How it's done:

1. If necessary, first trim the sprigs to the size of the bottles, then insert them inside the individual bottles. We used sprigs from pine, fir, box, and holly.

2. Finally, twist the candle into the neck of the bottle. To make sure it stands firmly in place, warm the wax at the bottom of the candle first.

✱ ❅ ❅
🕓 *10 minutes*

You will need:

* ✱ *secateurs*
* ✱ *various sprigs of evergreen foliage*
* ✱ *empty glass bottles*
* ✱ *candles*

"I will honour Christmas in my heart, and try to keep it all the year"

Charles Dickens

✱ Tip ✱

If your candles are prone to dripping, make sure you put something underneath to catch the molten wax.

Wrapping

Wooden boxes

These lovely and exceptionally practical round boxes can be found in any well-stocked craft shop.

* ❆ ❆

🕐 *1–5 minutes per box*

You will need:

* *wooden boxes*
* *acrylic paint in various colours*
* *paintbrush*
* *masking tape in gold and silver*

By adding a bit of colour, these containers can quickly be transformed into personalized gift boxes. There is no way these will be thrown away; they can simply be reused time after time. Here we've used our boxes for cookies and delicious baked treats, but of course they are just as good for jewellery or whatever gift you want to put inside. The boxes also stack nicely and so are an ideal storage system for all your essential little bits and pieces.

How it's done:

1. Paint the wooden boxes using acrylic paint in whatever colours you fancy: we used black, white, red, and yellow. You can paint them inside or outside, maybe just the lid, the same colour all over, or multi-coloured.

2. Festive masking tape – in gold or silver or other bright colours – makes a lovely decoration for the edge of the lid.

"The manner of giving is worth more than the gift"

Pierre Corneille

Decorating

Floating candles

This table decoration can be made in the twinkling of an eye. It is wonderfully festive as well as having a modern look, and you can coordinate the colour of the water to match your table setting.

The floating lights guarantee a relaxed atmosphere and a cosy mood at the table. What's more, you don't need to worry about the decoration catching fire, as it is already in water.

How it's done:

1. Fill the glass containers with water. Make sure the water levels vary.

2. Now add a couple of drops of colour to the water and mix to combine evenly.

3. Finally, float the candles on the water, putting 1 or more into each container before lighting them.

✱ ❀ ❀

🕑 *10 minutes*

You will need:

✱ *various glass containers*
✱ *liquid dye (food colouring, watercolours, silk paint, ink)*
✱ *floating candles*

✱ Tip ✱

Make sure you buy floating candles which burn for a long time, otherwise you will have to keep replacing them.

Giving

Bath salts

Bath salts are a lovely present for all those stressed-out people in the world… someone you love will probably need these!

This is a pampering gift which, in a sense, grants the recipient permission to give themselves a bit of "me" time. After all that Christmas stress, a hot bath ensures a proper dose of relaxation and recovery.

How it's done:

1. Mix the bath salts with a few dried rose petals and/or lavender flowers (use a proportion of roughly 1 handful of bath salts to 1 tsp petals) and put the mixture into a screw-top jar.

2. Tie raffia around the jar. Cover the lid with brown paper. Transfer the star template on to the silver coloured paper, cut out the star and stick this on the lid.

∗ ❋ ❋

🕐 *5 minutes*

You will need:

* ∗ *natural bath salts with no added substances*
* ∗ *dried rose petals and/ or lavender flowers*
* ∗ *teaspoon*
* ∗ *screw-top jar*
* ∗ *raffia*
* ∗ *brown paper*
* ∗ *template (see p122)*
* ∗ *silver coloured paper*
* ∗ *scissors*
* ∗ *all-purpose glue*

∗ Tip ∗

Take care to avoid getting the bath salts wet, so the mix doesn't clump together in the jar.

"The enigma of Christmas is that, on our quest for the great and the extraordinary, our attention is drawn to the inconsequential and the small"

Author unknown

Giving

Lavender bags

These fragrant and pretty pouches are the ideal little gift next time you are invited over by friends or family.

The lavender bags can be kept in your wardrobe among your winter jumpers and coats, to protect the clothes from moth damage. At the same time, they fill the closet with a lovely aroma.

How it's done:

1. Cut the fabric for each bag into a 28 × 10cm (11 × 4in) shape. Fold the piece widthways in the middle and sew up the sides (for tips on sewing, see pp107–109).

2. Now turn the bag, easing out the corners using the tips of the scissors, and fill with dried lavender flowers.

3. Finally, tie the bag at the top with a piece of lace trim.

✷ ❄ ❄

🕑 *5 minutes per bag*

You will need:

✷ *scissors*
✷ *white linen fabric, 28 × 10cm (11 × 4in) for each bag*
✷ *white thread*
✷ *sewing machine*
✷ *dried lavender flowers*
✷ *lace trim, 25cm (10in) for each bag*

✷ Tip ✷

If you are not a fan of the scent of lavender, you could also fill the bags with dried cloves or cinnamon sticks.

Wrapping

Apple cards

Beautiful notes which come from the heart don't have to be expensive, just really personal. A simple apple, plus a bit of red paint, and your Christmas post is ready to send!

∗ ❀ ❀

🕑 *1 minute per card*

You will need:

∗ *knife*
∗ *apple*
∗ *red acrylic paint*
∗ *little sponge*
∗ *white cards and envelopes*

The most memorable presents are little, hand-made gifts. Although this project is simple, the printed card is a one-off and far nicer, we think, than a shop-bought Christmas cards. The kids will love getting stuck in with this project, too!

How it's done:

1. Cut the apple lengthways through the middle.

2. Dab the cut surfaces with paint, using the little sponge, and use it as a stamp to decorate the cards and envelopes.

3. Leave to dry, write a heart-felt message… then post it off!

The apple is the predecessor of the Christmas tree bauble. As early as medieval times, trees would have been decorated with apples to represent the tree of life, from the biblical Garden of Eden. Later additions included lebkuchen (see p32) and nuts. After Twelfth Night, from 6 January, all the tree decorations could be eaten!

Techniques
&
templates

Sewing

*These sewing techniques will help you with
the projects on pages 42, 46, 62, and 102.*

Simple basting stitch

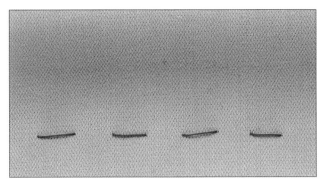

You work from right to left. Start with a knot on the end of a thread, thread the needle, then poke the needle in and out of the material at regular intervals.

Sewing machine straight stitch

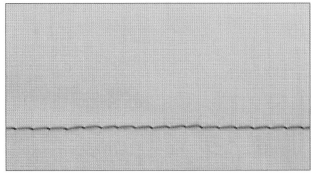

Most modern sewing machines can sew a variety of utility and decorative stitches as well as buttonholes. Straight stitch is suitable for most purposes. The stitch length can usually be adjusted up to 5mm (¼in).

Buttonhole stitch

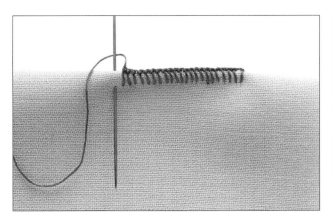

1. Sew narrow stitches from right to left over the edge of the fabric. The needle should come down vertically through the edge of the fabric.

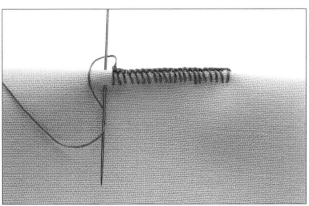

2. Arrange the thread behind the upper end of the needle and underneath the tip of the needle. When you pull the needle through, a knot will be created at the edge of the material to form a neat border effect.

Embroidery

These embroidery techniques will help with the project on page 26.

Running stitch

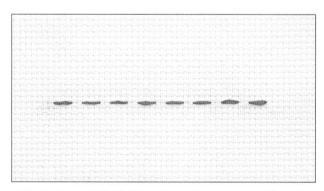

This simplest stitch of all can be used on any type of needlework project.

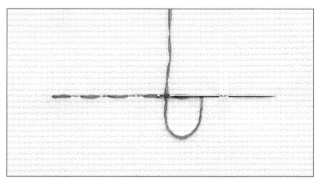

1. Take the needle in and out of the fabric along the line being stitched. Keep the stitch length even on top. Short stitches on the back will make the front stitches closer together and vice versa.

Backstitch

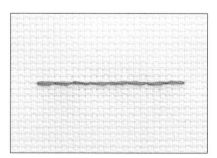

Backstitch creates a straight line without the spacing of running stitch.

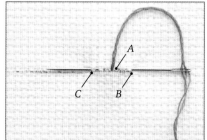

1. Work from right to left. Bring the needle out at A, one stitch length from the right-hand end of the guideline. Insert it at B, the end of the line. Come out at C, one stitch length in front of A.

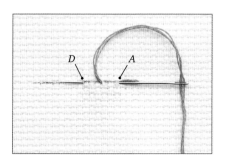

2. Insert at A again, and come out at D. Continue along the line.

Cross stitch

A single cross stitch is formed by two stitches crossing each other at an angle.

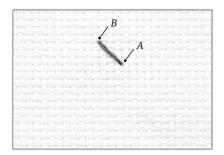

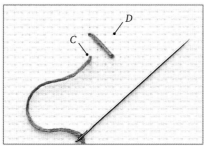

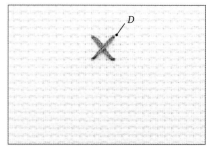

1. Bring the needle up on the base line at A and work one diagonal stitch to B, from bottom right to upper left.

2. Bring the needle up on the base line at C directly below the end of the first diagonal stitch.

3. To finish the cross, work another diagonal stitch to D, across the first one, in the opposite direction.

Serial cross stitch

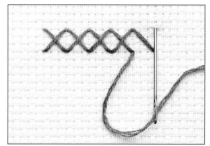

To work a row of neat cross stitches, keep the top and base of the stitch the same number of rows apart.

1. Work evenly spaced diagonal stitches in one direction to the end of the row.

2. Bring the needle up on the base line directly below the end of the last diagonal stitch. Work back in the opposite direction, making a row of diagonal stitches that crosses the first row.

Straight stitch

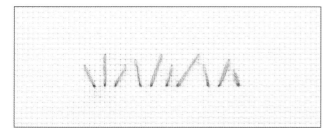

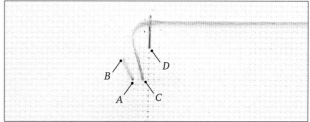

Also called stroke stitch or single satin stitch. The length, slant, and regularity can vary, but keep the stitching fairly short.

1. Bring the needle out at A and insert at B. Come out at C and insert at D. Repeat.

Knitting

These knitting techniques will help you with the projects on pages 46 and 70.

Single cast-on

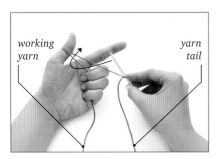

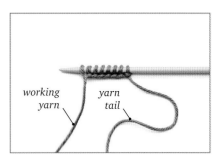

1. Hold the needle with the slip knot in your right hand. Place the wool, as shown, around your left thumb and hold it with your other fingers. Then take the needle around the thread in the direction shown by the arrow.

2. Let the yarn slip off your thumb and pull the yarn to tighten the new cast-on loop on the needle, sliding it up close to the slip knot.

3. Loop the yarn around your thumb again and repeat this process until you have as many stitches on the needle as required.

Knit-on cast-on

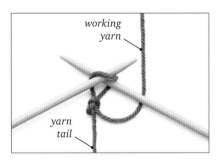

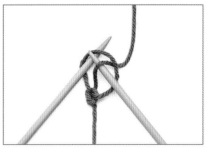

1. Place the needle with the slip knot on it in the left hand. Insert the tip of the right needle from right to left through the centre of the loop on the left needle, as shown.

2. With the yarn behind the needles, wrap it under and around the tip of the right needle. While casting on, use the left forefinger or middle finger to hold the loops on the left needle in position.

3. With the tip of the right needle, carefully draw the yarn through the loop on the left needle. This is the same way that knit stitch is formed.

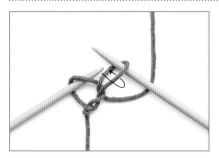

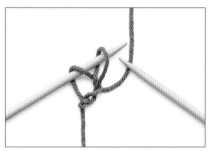

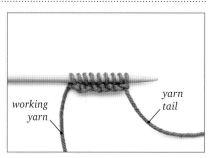

working
yarn

yarn
tail

4. Transfer the loop on the right needle to the left needle by inserting the tip of the left needle from right to left through the front of the loop.

5. Pull both yarn ends to tighten the new cast-on loop on the needle, sliding it up close to the slip knot.

6. Continue in this way until you have the required number of stitches.

Knit stitch

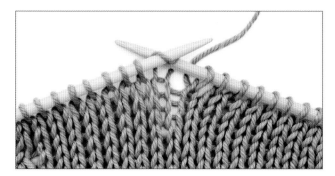

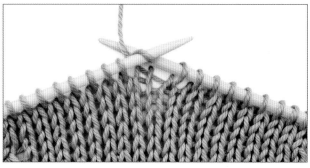

1. Hold the needle with the unworked stitches in your left hand and the other needle in your right hand. With the working yarn behind the needle, insert the right needle from left to right through the centre of the next stitch to be worked on the left needle

2. Wrap the yarn under and around the tip of the right needle, keeping an even tension on the yarn as it slips through your fingers.

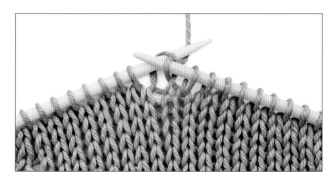

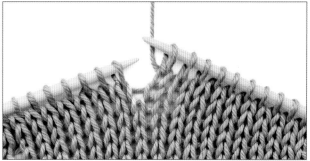

3. Catch the yarn with the tip of the right needle and carefully draw it through the stitch on the left needle. Try to hold the yarn firmly but not too tightly.

4. Let the old loop drop off the left needle to complete the stitch. Work all the stitches on the left needle onto the right needle in the same way to complete the row. Turn the work and transfer the right needle to the left hand.

Purl stitch

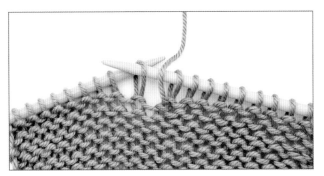

1. Hold the free working needle in your right hand. With the working yarn at the front of the knitting, insert the tip of the right needle from right to left through the centre of the next stitch to be worked on the left needle.

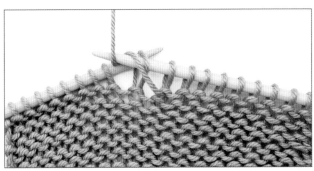

2. Wrap the yarn over and around the tip of the right needle. Try to keep an even tension on the yarn as you release the yarn through your fingers.

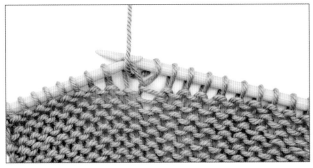

3. With the tip of the right needle, carefully draw the yarn through the stitch on the left needle. Keep you hands relaxed and allow the yarn to slip through your fingers in a gently controlled manner.

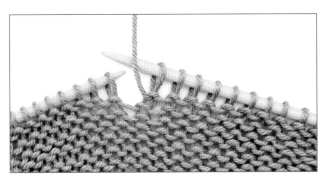

4. Let the old loop drop off the left needle to complete the stitch. Work all the stitches on the left needle onto the right needle in the same way to complete the row. To start the next row, turn the work and transfer the knitting to the left hand.

Garter stitch

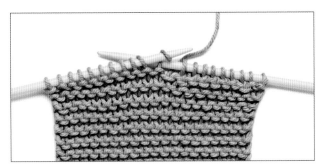

1. Garter stitch is worked entirely in knit stitch. The right and wrong sides look the same. When the right side of the fabric is facing you, knit all the stitches in the row.

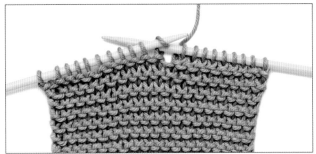

2. When the wrong side of the fabric is facing you, knit all the stitches in the row. The resulting fabric is soft, textured, and slightly stretchy with edges that lie flat.

Stocking stitch

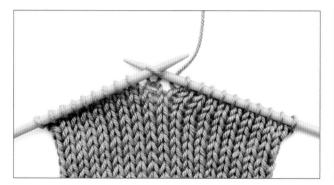

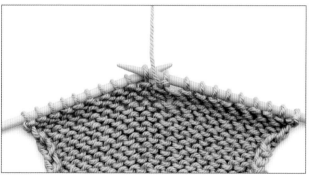

1. Stocking stitch is formed by working a row of knit stitches and a row of purl stitches alternately. When the right side of the fabric is facing you, as shown, knit all the stitches in the row.

2. When the wrong side of the fabric is facing you, as shown, purl all the stitches in the row. The wrong side is often referred to as the "purl side" of the knitting.

Tension square

Before beginning any knitting project, you should make a tension square. Depending how loosely or tightly you knit, you may need to use a different needle size in order to achieve the tension required by the pattern.

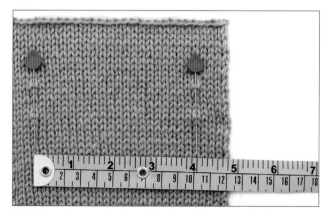

1. Using the specified needle size, knit a swatch about 13cm (5in) square. Mark 10cm (4in) across the centre of your swatch with pins and count the cumber of stitches between the pins.

2. Count the number of rows to 10cm (4in) in the same way. If you have fewer stitches and rows than you should, try again with a smaller needle size; if you have more, change to a larger needle size. Use the needle size for your knitting that best matches the correct tension given for your pattern.

Knit 2 stitches together

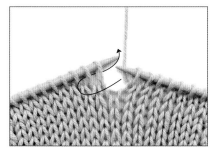 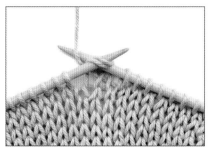 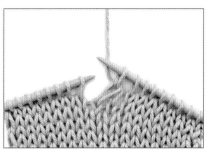

1. Insert the tip of the right needle from left to right through the second stitch then the first stitch on the left needle.

2. Wrap the yarn around the tip of the right needle, draw the yarn through both loops, and drop the old stitches off the left needle.

3. This makes two stitches into one and decreases one stitch in the row. The completed stitch slants right.

Knitting with five double-pointed needles

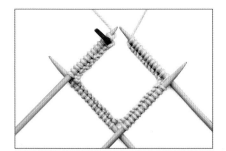  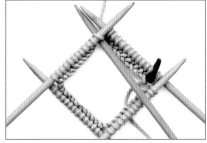

1. Cast on your stitches on a single needle, then distribute them across 4 double-pointed needles. Insert a stitch marker between the first 2 stitches on the first round. Arrange the needles to form a square, taking care not to twist your cast-on row.

2. You knit with the free, fifth needle. Knit the first stitch on each needle tightly to avoid gaps at the point where you transition from 1 needle to another.

3. When the stitches on the first needle have all been knitted, this becomes your working needle. Continue to knit in rounds slipping the stitch marker from the left to right needle when it is reached.

Knitting in moss stitch

Cast on an even number of stitches. On the right side, work knit 1, purl 1, alternating; on the wrong side, work purl 1, knit 1, again alternating. If you have an uneven number of stitches, you should simply knit 1, purl 1 on all rows to ensure you always end with a knit stitch.

Knitting with multiple colours
Two-colour garter stitch stripe

This narrow stripe pattern is worked in Garter stitch in two colours. To work the stripe, knit 2 rows in each colour alternately, dropping the colour not in use at the side of the work and picking it up again when it is needed.

Tidy edges

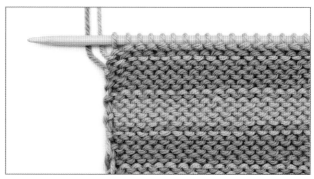

When working two coloured, even row stripes, twist the yarn around each other every 1–2cm (½–¾in) up the side of the piece. Alternating the direction of the twist after each colour change prevents the yarns becoming tangled. Be careful not to pull them tightly or the edge will pucker. This technique may make a bulky seam if used with more than two colours.

Weaving in the yarn ends

1. On right side rows it is possible to weave in ends as you knit. Start with the new colour held in the right hand, and the old colour over the left index finger. Insert the right needle into the first stitch, bring the old colour around front of right needle from right to left.

2. Bring the new colour between the needles and knit the stitch as normal. By doing this, the old colour yarn slips to the right and over the tip of the right needle, so it is not caught up as part of the new stitch. On the next stitch don't knit in the old yarn.

3. Repeat steps 1 and 2 until the old yarn end has been firmly secured. Knit until finished, then snip the yarn ends. Leave around 1cm (½in) hanging so that the ends don't slip through to the right side and become visible.

Crocheting

These crochet techniques will help you with the project on page 54.

Chain stitch

An initial chain (also called the foundation chain) made of chain stitches forms the basis of every crocheted item. Chain stitches are also needed for turning. In conjunction with other stitches, they produce a diverse range of open or closed stitch structures.

Chain stitch foundation chain

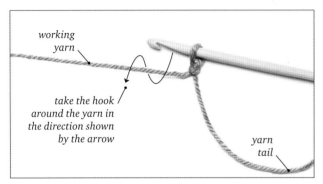

1. Start with a slip knot on your hook. Wrap the yarn around the hook. To do this, take the hook under the yarn and simultaneously pull the yarn slightly forwards.

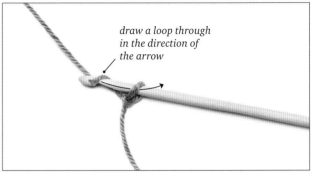

2. With the yarn caught in the lip of the hook, draw a loop of yarn through the loop on the hook shaft. Hold the base of the slip knot with the free fingers of your hand as you draw the loop through.

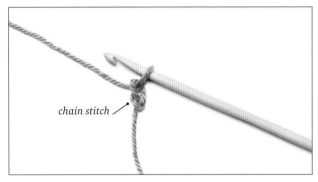

3. This completes the first chain stitch.

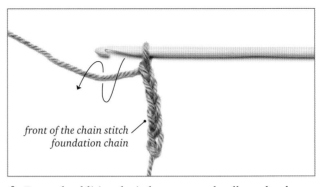

4. For each additional stitch, repeat and pull another loop through the stitch on the needle. Continue in this way until you have crocheted the specified number of chain stitches.

Counting chain stitches

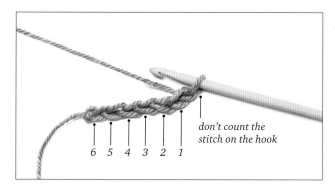

don't count the
stitch on the hook

6   5   4   3   2   1

Count along as you crochet until the desired number of chain stitches has been reached. Before you continue with your project, it's a good idea to check your numbers again. Hold the foundation chain with the right side towards you and count the stitches from the crochet hook to the left.

Double crochet

Double crochet is often used – either on its own or in combination with other stitches.

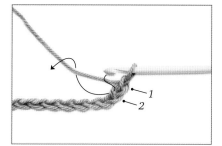

1
2

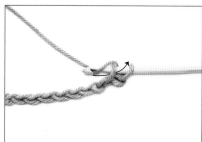

When double crochet is worked back and forth in rows it looks identical on both sides. If you work in rounds, the front and back of the work look different.

1. Crochet a foundation chain (see left) of the required length. Insert your hook through the second stitch from the hook and wrap the yarn around the hook following the arrow. Here the hook is inserted under a single strand, but you can also take the hook under 2 strands of yarn.

2. Hold the base of the foundation chain firmly in your left hand. Tension the yarn and draw a loop back through the chain stitch in the direction shown by the arrow. ➤➤

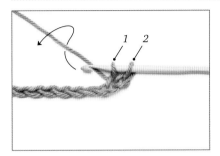

3. Now there are 2 loops on the crochet hook. Take the hook around the yarn in the direction shown by the arrow.

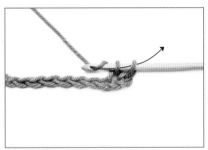

4. Pull the yarn loop through both stitches on the hook in one smooth action. Let the working yarn slide through your fingers but keep the yarn tension constant.

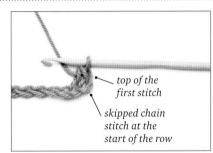

top of the first stitch

skipped chain stitch at the start of the row

5. The first double crochet stitch is complete. The skipped chain stitch at the start of the row is not counted as a stitch, it serves as a turning stitch.

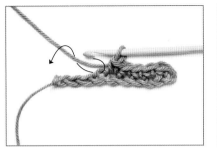

6. Work a double crochet stitch in each of the following chain stitches in the row in exactly the same way.

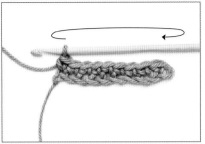

7. At the end of the row, turn the work so that the working yarn lies to the right. You can then begin the next row.

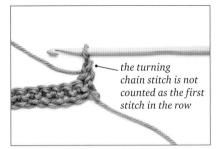

the turning chain stitch is not counted as the first stitch in the row

8. At the start of the second row, crochet a chain stitch. This is the turning stitch. It takes the yarn up to the correct level for the next row of double crochet stitches.

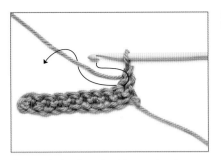

9. Work the first double crochet into the top of the first stitch in the row below. Work a double crochet into the top of each remaining double crochets in the row below.

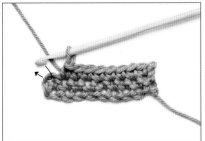

10. At the end of the row, work the last stitch into the top of the last double crochet of the row below. Work the following rows as for the second row.

11. When your piece is finished, cut the yarn, leaving a 10cm (4in) thread hanging. Remove the hook from the final stitch, bring the yarn end through, and pull the stitch firmly closed. This finishing technique is used for all stitch types.

Tension square

Before beginning a crochet project, make a tension square. Depending on how loosely or tightly you crochet, you may need to use a different hook size to achieve the tension specified in the pattern.

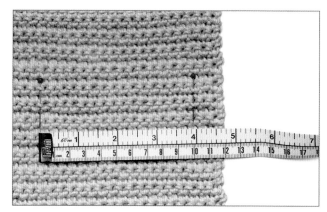

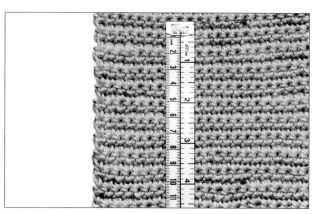

1. Using the specified hook, crochet a sample piece measuring about 13cm (5in) square. Insert 2 pins 10cm (4in) apart and count the stitches in between.

2. Count the rows over 10cm (4in) in the same manner. If there are fewer than specified in the pattern, try again with a slightly smaller crochet hook. If there are more, use a larger hook. Precision in the stitch width is more important than row height.

Double crochet increases

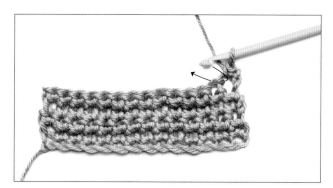

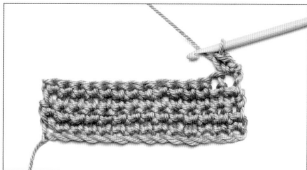

1. To increase one stitch at the beginning of a row of double crochet, work one double crochet stitch into the first stitch in the usual way. Next, insert the hook again into the first stitch and work a second double crochet in the same stitch.

2. This completes the increase. Proceed as usual, double crocheting into each double crochet stitch in the previous row. ➤➤

3. At the end of the row, work one double crochet stitch into the last stitch of the row in the usual way. Insert the hook again into the crochet stitch of the row and work a second double crochet stitch.

4. This increases once stitch at the end of the row.

Crocheting in the round using a loop

This crocheted loop is a quick and simple starting technique for flat shapes crocheted in the round. It lets you control the hole in the centre.

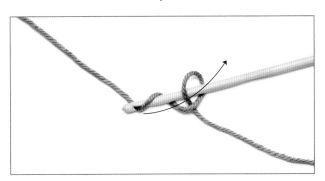

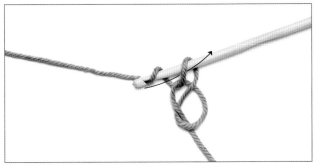

1. Form a loop from the yarn and pull the working thread through.

2. Don't pull the loop closed. To begin the first round, crochet a chain stitch into the loop.

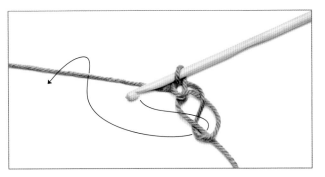

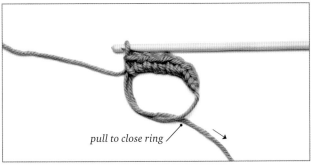

pull to close ring

3. Work the first round of double crochet stitches, working them into the ring and over the yarn tail as shown by the arrow.

4. When all of the required stitches are worked into the ring, pull the yarn tail to close the ring. Then continue as explained in the pattern instructions.

Pompoms and tassels

These pompoms and tassels are needed for the projects on pages 28 and 42.

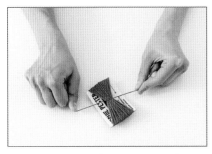

1. In both cases, first you wrap the wool around a small, strong piece of card. We used a business card. It's the ideal size.

2. To produce a tassel, you tie together the loops on 1 side of the card. To create a pompom, you tie together the loops on both sides of the card.

3. Slide the loops off the card. For the tassel (pink) you wrap a thread around all the loops just below where the ends are tied, bundling them together. This produces a little round "top knot".

4. For a pompom (red) you knot together the thread ends on both sides.

5. Finally, for both the tassel and the pompom, you cut the loops of wool at the bottom and neatly trim the threads to the correct length.

You can download all the templates from our website www.supercraftlab.com/downloads

Decorating

Christmas tree decorations: painted wooden discs

Template for the projects on pages 30, 38, and 100.

Snowflake tablecloth

Template for the project on page 26.
You will find embroidery tips on pages 108–109.

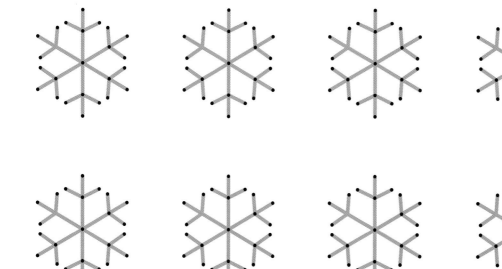

Giving

Advent calendar

Templates for the project on page 38.

Enlarge all templates by 150%, or to your required size.

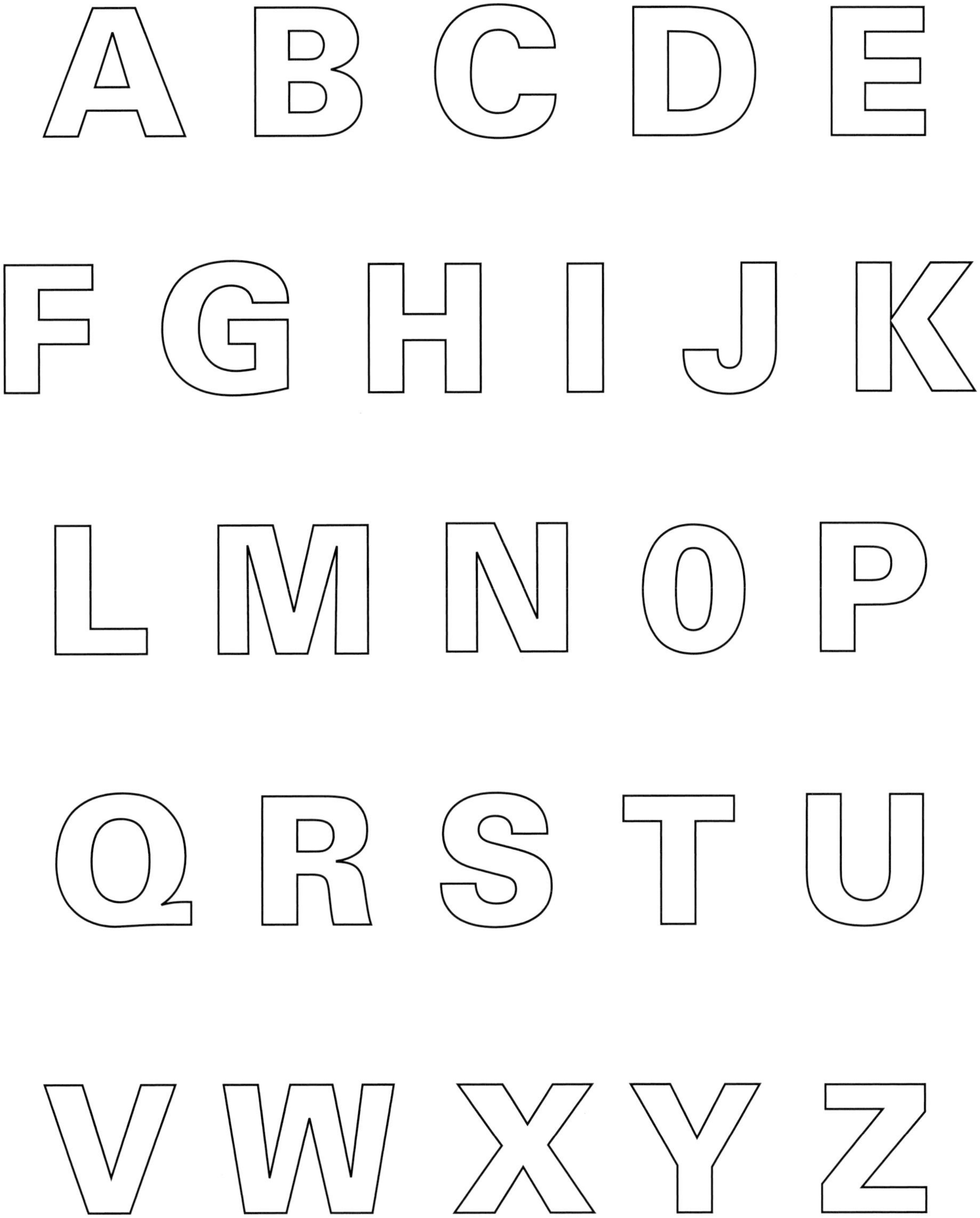

A B C D E

F G H I J K

L M N O P

Q R S T U

V W X Y Z

Good luck angel

Templates for the project on page 42.

Cosmetic bags

Pattern for the project on page 48.

Enlarge template by 150%. Note that the 2cm (¾in) seam allowance
is not taken into account in this pattern and will need to be added
when cutting out the lining material.

Family t-shirts

Templates for the project on page 50.
Enlarge all templates by 170%.

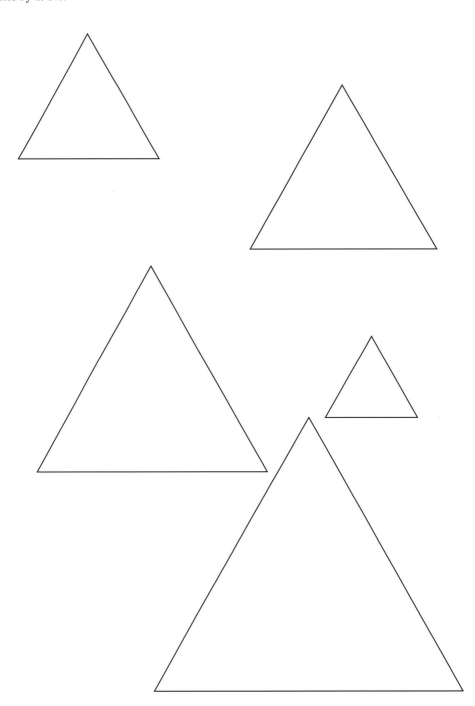

Typography picture

Templates for the project on page 60.
Enlarge all templates by 160%, or to your required size.

Kitchen apron

Pattern for the project on page 62.

Enlarge all templates by 475%.

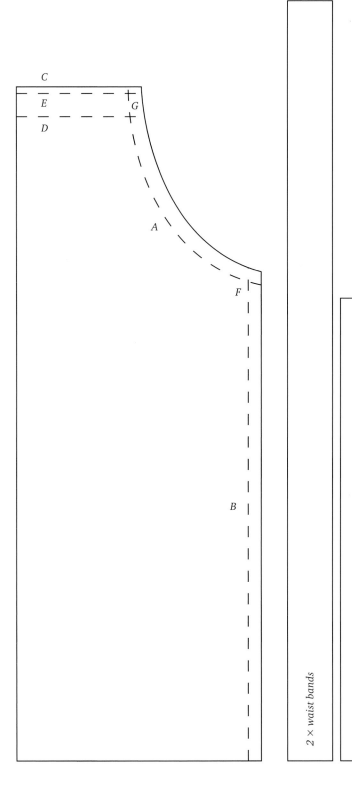

C

E

D

G

A

F

B

2 × waist bands

1 × neck loop

Packing

Festive gift wrap with paper bows

Templates for the project on page 76.
Enlarge all templates by 180%.

Rudolph gift wrap

Templates for the project on page 84.

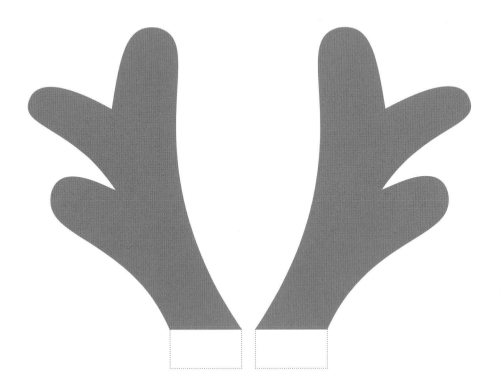

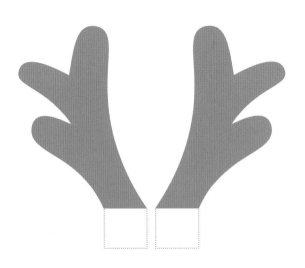

Gift bags

Templates for the project on page 86.

Manufacturers & suppliers

When selecting our materials we focus particularly on quality and on fair manufacturing conditions and, wherever possible, we support small businesses. Many of the materials and tools used in this book come from friendly labels or established wholesalers with whom we also love working. The following links will help you track down suppliers and buy any required materials online.

DIY kits, fabric, paper, paints: **www.supercraftlab.com**

Wool: **www.loveknitting.com**

Craft supplies: **www.homecrafts.co.uk**

Bakers twine: **www.beautiful-bakers-twine.com**

Art supplies: **www.cassart.co.uk**

DIY accessories: **www.diy.com**

Needlework supplies: **www.sewandso.co.uk**

Furniture and architecture: **www.questhardware.co.uk**

About the authors

Sophie Pester and Catharina Bruns are the founders of Supercraft, the DIY kits and materials shop for creative do-it-yourself enthusiasts. Not only are they both passionate designers and DIYers, they are also entrepreneurs and authors who are particularly involved in two related topics: do-it-yourself and entrepreneurship or, in other words, creative self-sufficiency. Their 'hello handmade' project is one of the most popular design markets in Germany. They founded Lemon Books, which is a design platform and manufacturing initiative for creating personalized notebooks, and they also launched the interview and workshop series 'superwork'. Behind all these initiatives there is one overriding goal: they want to inspire people to discover their own creative powers and self-sufficiency and give them the courage to do more themselves; whether that's handicraft hobbies or launching their own business.

www.supercraftlab.com
www.hello-handmade.com
www.lemonbooks.de
www.super-work.com
www.workisnotajob.com

Other books by the authors:
Supercraft – easy projects for every weekend also published by DK
Work is not a job – Was Arbeit ist, entscheidest du! and *Frei sein statt frei haben. Mit den eigenen Ideen in die kreative berufliche Selbstständigkeit*, both published by Campus

Acknowledgements

Thank you, dear readers, for choosing our book! We hope our ideas spur on your imaginations and provide you with plenty of inspiration for a creative Christmas.

Of course, we give special thanks to our many helpers, without whom this book would never have been so wonderful. Our sincere thanks go to:

* Sophie's dearest goddaughter Philippa Renz
* Sophie's best friend Susan Renz
* Our dear friends: Tom Sonntag, Ulrike Dix, and Patrick Sonntag
* Our crochet and knitting expert and kind supporter Christel Meyer
* Our supporter and expert sewer Ursula Heinrich
* The creative florist Bianca Pechstein
* Sophie's parents Ulrike and Andreas Pester for the lovely shooting location, the pretty Christmas decorative scene, delicious catering, and moral support
* Sophie's granny Christel Dittrich for her moral support

A massive thank you to our favourite photographer Anne Deppe (**www.annedeppe.de**) and to DK publishers, particularly to our editor Katharina May, for a fabulous collaboration.

Photography Anne Deppe
Editor Julia Niehaus
Designer Daniela Rudolf

For DK Germany

Publisher Monika Schlitzer
Managing Editor Caren Hummel
Project Manager Katharina May
Production Manager Dorothee Whittaker
Production Coordinator Arnika Marx
Production Christine Rühmer

For DK UK

Translator Alison Tunley
Editor Lucy Bannell
Senior Editor Kathryn Meeker
Senior Art Editor Glenda Fisher
Producer, Pre-production Catherine Williams
Senior Producer Stephanie McConnell
Creative Technical Support Sonia Charbonnier
Managing Editor Stephanie Farrow
Managing Art Editor Christine Keilty

First British Edition, 2017
Dorling Kindersley Limited
80 Strand, London, WC2R 0RL
A Penguin Random House company

A CIP catalogue record for this book is available from the British Library.
ISBN: 978-0-2412-9667-7

Printed and bound in China

A WORLD OF IDEAS:
SEE ALL THERE IS TO KNOW
www.dk.com